BUILDING

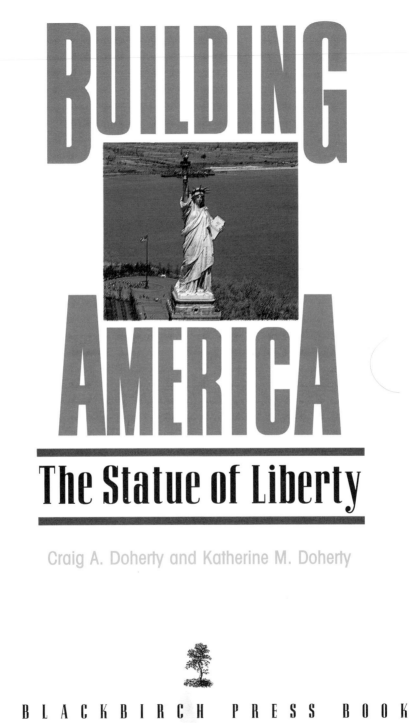

AMERICA

The Statue of Liberty

Craig A. Doherty and Katherine M. Doherty

A BLACKBIRCH PRESS BOOK

WOODBRIDGE, CONNECTICUT

To the memory of our friend, Donna Campbell

Special Thanks

The publisher would like to thank Barry Moreno and Jeffrey S. Dosik of the Statue of Liberty/Ellis Island National Monument for their help on this project.

Published by Blackbirch Press, Inc.
260 Amity Road
Woodbridge, CT 06525

© 1997 Blackbirch Press, Inc.
First Edition

Printed in the United States

10 9 8 7 6 5 4 3 2 1

Editorial Director: Bruce Glassman
Senior Editor: Nicole Bowen
Associate Editor: Elizabeth M. Taylor
Design and Production: Moore Graphics!

Photo Credits

Cover: ©Henryk T. Kaiser/Leo de Wys, Inc.; title page: ©Henryk T. Kaiser/Leo de Wys, Inc.; contents page: (from top to bottom) ©Everett Johnson/Leo de Wys, Inc.; Library of Congress; The Bettman Archive; Statue of Liberty National Monument; ©Steve Ross/Leo de Wys, Inc. Page 4: ©Everett Johnson/Leo de Wys, Inc.; pages 6, 11, 12 (top), 13, 14, 15, 17, 20, 21, 23, 26, 27, 28, 32, 37 (bottom left), 38, 39, 41: by courtesy of the Statue of Liberty National Monument; pages 8, 9, 12, 37 (top): Library of Congress; page 10: Services Culturels Français; page 18, 19, 22 (bottom): The Bettmann Archive; page 22 (top): National Portrait Gallery; pages 23, 29, 30: North Wind Picture Archives; page 31: ©Dick Luria/Leo de Wys, Inc.; page 33: Reuters/Bettmann; page 34, 35: ©Steve Ross/Leo de Wys, Inc.; page 37 (bottom right): New York State Department of Economic Development; pages 40, 42–43: ©Henryk T. Kaiser/Leo de Wys, Inc.

Library of Congress Cataloging-in-Publication Data

Doherty, Craig A.
  The Statue of Liberty / by Craig A. Doherty and Katherine M. Doherty.
      p. cm.—(Building America)
  Includes bibliographical references and index.
  Summary: A history of the Statue of Liberty with an emphasis on the basic architecture, engineering, and mechanical procedures of construction.
  ISBN 1-56711-111-4 (lib. bdg.:alk. paper)
  1. Statute of Liberty (New York, N.Y.)—Juvenile literature. 2. New York (N.Y.)—Buildings, structures, etc.—Juvenile literature. [1. Statue of Liberty (New York, N.Y.) 2. National monuments.] I. Doherty, Katherine M. II. Title. III. Series: Doherty, Craig A. Building America.
  F128.64.L6D64 1997   95-20921
  974.7'1—dc20   CIP
                                            AC

Table of Contents

INTRODUCTION...5

CHAPTER 1   Building the Statue........................9

CHAPTER 2   The American-Made Pedestal.......19

CHAPTER 3   Liberty Rises Above the Harbor....27

CHAPTER 4   Liberty Gets a Face-Lift.................35

GLOSSARY...44

CHRONOLOGY...45

FURTHER READING.....................................46

SOURCE NOTES..46

INDEX...47

Introduction

One of the most recognizable landmarks in the world is the Statue of Liberty. For more than 100 years Liberty has stood holding her torch high as a symbol of the freedom and independence that the United States represents to the world. How the statue came to stand on an island in New York Harbor is an important story in the building of America.

In 1776, thirteen British colonies in North America banded together and declared their independence from England. The American Revolution followed, and the only country to come to the aid of the young United States was France, England's long-time rival. This bond between France and the United States was strengthened when the French people followed

Opposite: Since 1886, the Statue of Liberty has held her torch over New York Harbor.

Frenchman Edouard-René Lefebvre de Laboulaye was the first to develop the idea of a gift from the people of France to the people of America. This gift would be the Statue of Liberty.

the lead of their American counterparts and revolted against the French monarchy in 1789.

As the centennial of the Declaration of Independence approached, a group of French people, led by Edouard-René Lefebvre de Laboulaye, decided that they should do something to honor the bond between the people of France and the people of the United States. Laboulaye was the foremost French authority on the history of the U.S. Constitution. It was at a dinner party hosted by Laboulaye in 1865 that the idea of a gift to the American people was first discussed.

One of the guests at the dinner was the talented and successful French sculptor Frédéric-Auguste Bartholdi. Bartholdi had a strong desire to do a monumental sculpture. He had traveled to Egypt and was influenced by the great works of the ancient Egyptians. He had even tried to convince the ruler of Egypt that he should have Bartholdi create a lighthouse in the form of a woman holding a torch at the mouth of the Suez Canal, which was just being built at the time.

Over the next five years, Bartholdi and Laboulaye held onto the idea of an American monument, and in 1870, Bartholdi completed the first model of the Statue of Liberty. The model was well received in France, and the following year, 1871, Bartholdi made a trip to the United States to look for a site to place the massive sculpture he envisioned. He traveled extensively in the United States, even riding the recently completed transcontinental railroad to San Francisco. Of all the places he visited in the United States, he thought the most appropriate for Liberty was one of the first places he had seen as his ship entered New York Harbor: Bedloe's Island. This was the site of Fort Wood, the eventual spot where Liberty would stand.

In 1875, the Franco-American Union was established to raise the money it would take to build the Statue of Liberty. The French committee of the union would raise the money for the statue, and their American counterparts would take care of building a pedestal on which to erect it. The fund-raising for the statue went well, and money came in from all over France. One-hundred-and-eighty-one towns and cities donated money, and thousands of school children and adults contributed what they could. In the first year, the union sent more than 14,000 subscription blanks to donors. Japy Frères, a large company that sold metal, donated the copper that would be used to cover Liberty. All who donated shared one common thought: They believed in the ideals of liberty for which the statue was to stand.

Building the Statue

In 1875, Bartholdi completed the final model of Liberty, and he could now begin to work on the actual statue. Because the finished statue would be 151-feet-and-1-inch tall— about 15 stories—Bartholdi planned to build it in sections. At Laboulaye's dinner party, the idea had been to have a monument to present to the American people for the 1876 centennial, the 100th anniversary of the Declaration of Independence. There was no way that the statue could be finished and ready to present in just one year. It would take almost nine years to complete Liberty. Bartholdi and the workers of Gaget, Gauthier, and Company—a Paris metal-working firm that was well known for working on large sculptures—were able to build Liberty's right arm and the torch for 1876. The arm and torch were

Opposite: *Liberty's arm and torch were put on display at the Philadelphia Centennial Celebration in 1876. The rest of the statue was not completed until eight years later.*

9

THE ARTIST, THE POLITICIAN, AND THE ENGINEER

A project the size of the Statue of Liberty required the efforts of many dedicated people with a variety of backgrounds. Obviously the sculptor, Frédéric-Auguste Bartholdi, was the creative force in the creation of Liberty, however, he could not have completed the sculpture alone. Edouard-René Lefebvre de Laboulaye organized the project and raised the money, while Alexandre-Gustave Eiffel engineered the frame that supported Liberty's copper skin.

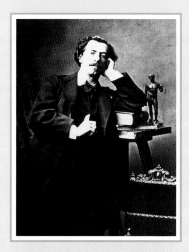

Bartholdi, about 1857

Frédéric-Auguste Bartholdi was born on August 2, 1834, in Colmar, a town in the Alsace province of eastern France. Bartholdi's father died when Auguste was only two. It had been his father's hope that his son would become a lawyer, however, his mother allowed him to pursue his dream of becoming an artist. After studying architecture, Bartholdi's interests turned to painting and, then, to sculpture. His passion for completing Liberty was, in part, caused by the political events of his lifetime. In 1870, Bartholdi joined the army of Napoléon III and experienced the defeats of the Franco-Prussian War. His home province of Alsace, and the province next to it, Lorraine, were taken over by the Prussians. The Prussians also kept an army of occupation in France for two years after the end of the war. At that time, some politicians in France were fighting to reestablish the republican form of government that had been adopted briefly after the French Revolution.

One of the leaders of the movement to reestablish the republic in France was Laboulaye. It was because of the political battles that he was fighting that Liberty was put on hold for a

sent to the Philadelphia Centennial Celebration and put on display. After the celebration was over in Philadelphia, the right arm and torch were sent to New York where they were set up in Madison Square. They remained there as a promise of what was to come until being sent back to France in 1884 to be added to the rest of the statue.

number of years after he and Bartholdi first came up with the idea. Laboulaye, and the other republicans were struggling with those who wanted to restore a monarchy in France. The defeat and exile of Napoléon III by the Prussians heightened the debate. Eventually, Laboulaye and his party succeeded, and he was elected senator for life. Throughout his writings and speeches of the time there was one impassioned theme, and that was liberty for the people of France.

Liberty, the statue, was important to him because it was through his study of the U.S. Constitution that he found his inspiration to fight for the rights of "life, liberty, and the pursuit of happiness."

For Laboulaye and Bartholdi, the ideal of liberty was a driving force in the creation of the statue. For Alexandre-Gustave Eiffel, the engineer who helped make it possible, the statue was much more of an engineering challenge than an expression of beliefs. Eiffel had made his reputation building railroad bridges and other iron structures.

Alexandre-Gustave Eiffel, 1885

In designing iron bridges, Eiffel was at the forefront of engineering ideas of the time. His greatest bridge spanned the Truyère River in south-central France. The bridge was more than 1,600 feet long and almost 400 feet above the river. The central span was more than 525 feet long. All of this was supported by an iron framework similar to the one that would go inside Liberty. Eiffel's most famous display of his iron-working skills is the tower in Paris that bears his name. The Eiffel Tower was built for the Paris Exhibition of 1889 and has become a landmark that is recognized throughout the world.

Without any one of these men, the Statue of Liberty would probably never have been completed. In addition to these three, tens of thousands of other people share in the success of Liberty. Workers in Paris and New York did their part, and thousands of people in both France and the United States believed enough in Liberty to make a financial contribution.

The size of the statue created a number of engineering problems for Bartholdi. Liberty is made of a copper skin that is ³/₃₂" thick over an iron frame. Although ³/₃₂" seems thin, more than 100 tons of copper make up the exterior of the statue. It would take a very strong frame to support the copper exterior. In 1879, Alexandre-Gustave Eiffel, the engineer who

later built the Eiffel Tower in Paris, joined Bartholdi and designed the iron skeleton for the statue.

The process of building a statue that is more than 150 feet tall requires a variety of complex steps. It begins with a number of plaster models, each proportionally larger than the one that came before it. The first model had been only four feet tall. The next model was one sixteenth the size of the finished statue, or just under 9½ feet. After Bartholdi was satisfied that every aspect of the one-sixteenth model was the way he wanted it, he and his crew went on to build a one-quarter scale model. This model stood almost 38 feet tall and was protected by a special shed.

The full-size model would have to be built in a number of sections because it was so massive. To do this accurately was of critical importance, so a system of measuring the one-quarter scale model was devised. A wooden frame was built around the model, which placed it inside a cube. From this cubic frame, three-dimensional measurements were taken, allowing the exact location of any part of the one-quarter model to be transferred to the full-size version. Thousands of measurements were taken from the one-quarter model, multiplied by four. These measurements were then applied to the sections of the full-size model.

Top:
Models were made in various sizes.
Bottom:
Plaster is applied to a mold of the hand.

Once the sections of the full-size model were completed, Bartholdi and the workers could move on to the next step. The ³⁄₃₂" copper skin of the statue was to be formed using a technique known as repoussé ("reh-pu-say"). When forming the skin of a statue using this method, the copper sheets are hammered into shape from the inside. To do this, the carpenters at Gaget, Gauthier, and Company first had to make wooden forms that exactly fit the shape of the full-size model sections. The copper was then shaped using the wooden frames.

The statue was such a large project that work progressed on more than one section at a time. The right arm and torch were the first to be finished. Then the head was done. Liberty's head was displayed at the 1878 Paris Universal Exposition, where people were allowed to go inside it for a fee. The money was used to keep the work going on the rest

Workers hammered copper sheets into exact forms made from the full-size model to create the statue's skin.

Top:
Liberty's head was
displayed in the
Champs de Mars,
in Paris, 1878.
Bottom:
The iron tower rises
on a Paris street.

of the statue. Some parts of the statue were even contracted out to firms outside of Paris. For example, one of the fingers was made to Bartholdi's specifications by a coppersmith in Montauban, in the southern part of France.

Liberty Rises in Paris

While Bartholdi and the copper-smiths formed the outer layer of the sculpture, work progressed on the frame that would support it. Eiffel was well known as a designer of innovative iron railroad bridges, and he used the knowledge that he had gained building bridges to design the supporting structure for Liberty. The building of the iron tower employed theories and techniques that would soon allow designers to build skyscrapers.

Eiffel and Bartholdi had to work very closely so that the tower and the outer skin would fit together. One problem that they had to deal with was the right arm and torch. In the models, the angle of the arm was too great to be supported by the iron work. Eiffel suggested that the arm be raised in a more vertical line from the body so that the stress of the projecting framework would be more manageable.

Outside the shops of Gaget, Gauthier, the supporting tower rose above the neighboring Paris buildings while the completed sections of the copper skin lay about the yards and shops. Visitors, who came to see how the work progressed, found it disorienting to see a foot lying in one corner, the completed head somewhere else.

Attaching all the pieces to each other was a complex job. The 350 individual sheets of copper had to be joined together using more than 300,000 rivets. (A rivet is a bolt or pin, in this case made of copper, with a head on one end. It is placed in holes in the materials to be joined together, then the other end of the pin is hammered down to hold the two pieces together tightly.) The coppersmiths used a variety of different style joints to attach the copper sheets to each other. In some areas of the statue, the edges of the copper sheets were beveled and then riveted, making an almost invisible seam. Beveling the edges was a difficult and time-consuming process in which the edges of the sheets were thinned on an angle so that they would perfectly overlap the sheets to which they were attached. The workers would then rivet the two beveled edges

The construction of the Statue of Liberty was a huge project. Many workers were involved, both in France and in the United States.

together. Various joints—such as butt joints, dovetail joints, and lap joints—were used in other areas.

The type of joint used depended on which area of the statue it was needed. In areas that needed to look smooth, such as the face, the joints had to be almost invisible, so they were beveled. In areas like the folds of Liberty's robes, simpler butt joints and lap joints were acceptable.

Once the sheets of copper were riveted together, an iron framework had to be attached to them. This framework served two purposes: First, it helped the copper sheets maintain their shape, and, second, it gave the workers something to attach to the iron skeleton of the statue. The use of iron and copper together in the statue created two problems for Bartholdi and Eiffel. Copper and iron expand and contract at different rates when the temperature changes, therefore, they could not be secured to each other. The other problem had to do with the possibility of the two metals reacting and causing the iron to corrode rapidly.

The first problem was solved by using copper brackets that held the copper sheets in place on the iron frame, while allowing for the differences in expansion and contraction. The problem of corrosion was solved by using asbestos coated with shellac as an insulator between the iron supports and the copper sheets.

Once the tower was built, it was time to start assembling Liberty in Paris. In and around the workshops of Gaget, Gauthier, the completed pieces were strewn around like a giant three-dimensional jigsaw puzzle. The completed head was in one corner, the

torch and right arm in another, and pieces of the statue's robe were everywhere. In 1881, the first piece of
the puzzle to be attached to Liberty's frame was the
big toe. By August 1884, the Statue of Liberty stood
tall and proud on a back street in Paris, France.

The American-Made Pedestal

The selection of the site for Liberty was very limited. The statue was so large that it had to be in a spot where it could be viewed from afar. Bartholdi had been offered two possibilities in New York Harbor: Bedloe's Island and Governor's Island. He chose Bedloe's because it was more isolated and smaller. The small size of the island, 12 acres, would make the statue appear even larger than it was. Also, the location of the island would allow Bartholdi to place the statue so it faced out to sea, greeting the tens of thousands of people who came through the Verrazano Narrows into New York Harbor.

Opposite:
A view of New York Harbor from Staten Island. Visible on the left is Bedloe's Island, the eventual site of the Statue of Liberty.

19

EMMA LAZARUS AND "THE NEW COLOSSUS"

During the fund-raising for the statue in the United States, many artists, writers, and poets were asked to donate works to be auctioned off. The proceeds of this auction were used to help build the pedestal. William M. Evarts, the head of the American committee, asked Emma Lazarus if she would write a poem for the auction. At first, Lazarus said no because she felt, as a serious poet, she could not write a poem to order. As she gave the subject more thought, however, a poem began to form in her mind.

Lazarus's family had first arrived in the mid-1600s. They had been one of the first Jewish families to immigrate to this "new" land. Her father owned a sugar refinery in New York, and Lazarus had been raised like many children of the wealthy at the time. She had been educated by private tutors and, at the age of 16, published her first book of poems.

In the late 1870s, Lazarus became concerned with the plight of Jews who were being persecuted in Russia. Because of the problems of Russia, many of them were immigrating to the United States. Lazarus visited the immigration station at Castle Garden at the tip of Manhattan. She was upset by conditions there and became active in the Hebrew Emigrant Aid

Emma Lazarus

Fort Wood had been built on the island between 1808 and 1811, but it had never seen any action. The fort was built in the shape of an 11-pointed star, and Bartholdi felt the fort could be incorporated into the base of the monument. The army had used the fort as a recruiting station during the Civil War but after the war had no use for it—they were planning to abandon it. Choosing the site, however, was much easier than preparing it for the statue.

Immigrants arriving at Castle Garden, 1880

Society. It is probably from these experiences and concerns that Lazarus found the inspiration for her poem written in 1883.

Lazarus usually rewrote her poems over and over again until she was satisfied that they were just right. "The New Colossus" was different. She wrote it in one sitting and never felt the need to rewrite the sonnet. Lazarus died of cancer in 1887, at 38.

Her poem was not well known at first, however, in 1903, a plaque was placed inside the pedestal of the statue with her words inscribed on it. Now the last lines of the poem are known by many. They speak to the promise that the United States has offered to people from all parts of the world.

THE NEW COLOSSUS

Not like the brazen giant of Greek fame,
with conquering limbs astride from land
   to land;
Here at our sea-washed, sunset gates
   shall stand
a mighty women with a torch, whose flame
is the imprisoned lightning, and her name
Mother of exiles. From her beacon-hand
glows world-wide welcome; her mild eyes
   command
the air-bridged harbor that twin cities frame.

"Keep, ancient lands, your storied
   pomp!": cries she
with silent lips. "Give me your tired, your
   poor,
your huddled masses yearning to
   breathe free,
The wretched refuse of your teeming shore.
Send these, the homeless, tempest-
   tost to me.
I lift my lamp beside the golden door!"

Raising the Money

People in the United States were not as interested in the great statue project as the people of France had been. Raising the money to build a suitable base for the statue turned into a major obstacle. By the time Bartholdi had completed the statue in Paris, only $16,000 of the $300,000 needed for the base had been raised. It seemed, for a period of time, that Liberty would have no place to stand.

Top:
Grover Cleveland
Bottom:
Joseph Pulitzer

Many different tactics were used to get the American public to support the statue. One successful effort involved the selling of replica statues that had been designed by Bartholdi. Bronzed miniatures standing on a nickel-silver base were sold in two sizes: The six-inch replica sold for one dollar, the 12-inch one sold for five dollars. Other attempts at fundraising were not as successful. Both the New York and federal legislatures attempted to raise money to help build the base. In Albany, Grover Cleveland, the governor, vetoed a $50,000 appropriation for the statue's pedestal. In Washington, the supporters of a bill to give $100,000 to the effort lost out. As Bartholdi and his workers started the difficult process of dismantling Liberty and packing up the pieces so they could be sent by ship to America, the prospects for the statue looked bleak in New York.

Joseph Pulitzer, the owner and publisher of the New York newspaper the *World*, can be considered the champion of the Statue of Liberty project in New York. Pulitzer was a Hungarian who had immigrated to the United States at the age of 17 and volunteered to fight for the Union during the last few months of the Civil War. After the war, Pulitzer, who spoke German, moved to St. Louis and got a job on a German language newspaper, the *Westliche Post*. Pulitzer went on to own the *Post-Dispatch* in St. Louis and the *World*, among many other newspapers. As a recent immigrant, Pulitzer appreciated the values that Liberty was intended to represent, and he used his papers to save the statue project in New York.

Pulitzer began his campaign by attacking the wealthy people of New York who had failed to support the statue. When this attack fell on deaf ears, Pulitzer decided to take the cause of the statue to the people of the country. His papers began running editorials calling for everyone to help. Pulitzer promised to publish the names of every contributor no matter how small their donation. The response was amazing: In the first week $2,000 arrived at the *World*. A kindergarten class in Iowa sent $1.35; in New Jersey 12 schools worked together and raised more than $100; an office boy in New York wrote a letter and sent in a nickel. Within five months, Pulitzer had raised more than $100,000, with the money coming from over 120,000 contributors! Pulitzer would eventually raise even more money for the statue, but the first $100,000 got the work started on Bedloe's Island.

Work Begins on the Base

The committee in charge of the pedestal commissioned Richard Morris Hunt, one of America's top architects of the time, to design the base. Hunt corresponded with Bartholdi and was sent all the artistic and engineering information that he would need to design the structure. Hunt's final design was readily accepted by the committee. The design called for the use of a relatively new material: concrete, which is a mixture of sand, cement, and small stones.

Large crowds gathered to watch as the cornerstone for the base was set in position.

When it is reinforced with steel bars, it is stronger than stone. Hunt's pedestal design would be the largest concrete structure made at the time. It would weigh more than 27,000 tons and would raise the total height of the statue to 305 feet, making it the tallest human-made structure in the world when finished.

When work began on the pedestal in 1883, the committee hired General Charles P. Stone to oversee the construction. General Stone was a Civil War veteran who had met Bartholdi while he was directing military operations for the Egyptian government in the Sudan in 1869. General Stone had been involved in a number of large construction projects and was a popular choice for the job.

The first task on Bedloe's Island was the excavation of the foundation for the pedestal, which was to be set in the center of Fort Wood. The base of the pedestal was designed to be 53 feet tall and 91 feet square at the bottom, which tapered to 65 feet square. The bottom of the base was set 17 feet below ground level. As the excavation began, the construction workers discovered that Fort Wood had been erected over a much earlier fort, probably built by the Dutch. The stonework of the earlier fort had to be removed, but the 11-pointed-star-

THE OTHER STATUE OF LIBERTY

As Bartholdi and his workers disassembled Liberty and packed her up for the move to the United States, many people in Paris were sad to see her go. A group of Americans who were living in Paris at the time decided to do something about it. In 1885, they collected enough money to have a one-quarter-size bronze replica of Liberty cast, which they donated to the people of France. The statue was placed on the Île des Cygnes (Island of Swans) in the Seine River in Paris. It still stands there today as a reminder of the bond that exists between the two countries and of the gift that the people of France gave to the people of the United States.

shaped walls of Fort Wood were allowed to stand and were later filled in.

Building the base was a big undertaking that required a large work force and a lot of equipment. A steam-powered derrick was set up in front of the pedestal. This derrick was used to hoist the materials for the pedestal, and later, its cables were used to raise the hundreds of pieces of Liberty into place.

Hunt's design called for the concrete base to be faced with granite. The granite came by boat from Leete's Island, in Connecticut. All of the materials for the statue had to be transported to Bedloe's Island by boat. A steamboat was bought to do most of the hauling for the project. It was renamed the *Bartholdi*.

The committee finally raised enough money to finish the base, only to realize they didn't have enough money to reerect the statue, which had arrived from France. Grover Cleveland, who had become the twenty-second president of the United States in 1885, agreed to ask Congress for $56,500 to complete the Statue of Liberty and hold a dedication ceremony. Congress approved the appropriation.

Opposite Top: Building the base required a large work force. Middle: At the time it was built, the pedestal was the largest concrete structure in the world. Bottom: The base raised the height of the statue to 305 feet.

Liberty Rises
Above the Harbor

The arrival of Liberty aboard the French ship *Isère* on June 17, 1885, had been announced in the newspapers, and more than 90 ships turned out to greet the statue. The actual assembly had to wait until the pedestal was completed early in 1886. Once work began, it went quickly. Eiffel's tower was attached to massive steel beams embedded deep within the base, and the same steam-powered derrick that had been used for the pedestal was put to work lifting the pieces of Liberty's iron skeleton.

The cable from the derrick, which was on the ground in front of the base, went into the entryway of the pedestal and up the elevator shaft to the top of the base. From there, it went to the derrick booms on the top of the iron work. It took precise signaling

Opposite:
Liberty was shipped to the United States in pieces and then reassembled.

27

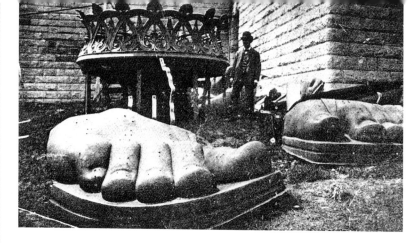

*Top:
Liberty's feet and
part of the torch
sit on Bedloe's
Island, waiting
for reassembly.*

*Bottom:
When the
statue was
reassembled
in New York,
workers put
the tower and
the copper skin
together at the
same time. It was
a difficult and
dangerous job.*

from the workers on the statue to the cable operator on the ground to control objects that were being hoisted up onto the statue.

A team of 75 workers reassembled Liberty in six months. It was difficult and dangerous work: The workers had to hang from ropes as they fitted the frame and the copper plates together. All 30,000 rivets that fastened the copper plates to each other had to be hammered tight, with one worker inside the statue and another on the outside. When the monument had originally been erected, the entire frame had been completed before the copper was hung. The workers who installed the copper skin during the reassembly followed the frame assemblers up the statue.

Because it was so tall—and because it stood out in open water—the metal statue would attract lightning. To deal with this, the copper skin of the statue was thoroughly grounded, allowing electricity from a lightning strike to pass through the skin into the ground. This system has worked well. Liberty has been hit by lightening many times, but the statue has never been damaged.

The Dedication

By the fall of 1886, Liberty was complete and standing as the tallest human-made structure in the world at that time. Although some art critics were unimpressed with the statue, most people found it a stirring tribute to the ideals of liberty and freedom. The dedication ceremony on October 28, 1886, drew a huge fleet of boats out into the harbor to view the statue and watch the nighttime fireworks display.

Bartholdi had made the trip from France to attend the dedication, and October 28 was officially declared Bartholdi Day in New York City. The sculptor was given a golden key to the city and taken to the nicest restaurant in town. Mr. Gaget, of Gaget, Gauthier, and Company, also came for the dedication. He brought three large trunks full of miniature Libertys. They were so popular that soon everyone

Fireworks explode over the many boats that gathered on October 28, 1886, for the Statue of Liberty's dedication.

Bartholdi had not originally planned on people going up in the statue. However, this was such a hit at the dedication that it was made a permanent option.

wanted one of those "gadget" statues, a phrase that entered a new word into American slang.

President Cleveland toured the harbor on the naval ship U.S.S. *Dispatch* as it reviewed the more than 300 ships and boats that crowded the water to attend the dedication ceremony. On land, 20,000 people marched in the dedication parade down Fifth Avenue and Broadway.

When it came time for the speeches, Ferdinand-Marie de Lesseps—the man who had taken the leadership responsibilities for the Franco-American Union when Laboulaye had died in 1884—spoke first. William M. Evarts, Lesseps's American counterpart, spoke next. The French flag covering Liberty's face was to be dropped at the end of his speech. Bartholdi was up in the statue ready to drop the flag, and a boy was down on the speakers' platform waiting to signal the end of the speech. Part way through his speech, Evarts made a rather long pause and, thinking the speech was over, the boy signaled Bartholdi. The flag dropped, every boat surrounding the island blew its horn, and the navy began its 21-gun salute. The speech was never completed.

For the dedication, visitors were allowed to go up in the statue. The wooden staircase that wound up through the skeleton had been built for workers and to assemble and maintain the structure. Bartholdi had not planned on visitors climbing up inside the statue, but this proved to be so popular that the wooden staircase was soon replaced by a double, iron, spiral staircase. Each staircase has 171 steps, one for going up, the other for coming down. The inside of the statue has been open to tourists since the first day, except during maintenance.

Maintaining Liberty

Deciding who would be responsible for the care and maintenance of Liberty was a problem from the earliest days. The first custodian of the statue was the Lighthouse Board, a federal agency that kept and maintained lighthouses along the coasts and waterways of the United States. But Liberty was not made into a lighthouse, so the Lighthouse Board transferred responsibility for the structure to the War Department, which still owned all of Bedloe's Island except for the two acres on which the statue stood. In 1933, Liberty's care was transferred to the National Park Service, which continues to oversee it today.

Over the years, various maintenance jobs have been done on the statue. In 1907, new granite facings were added to the pedestal and the skeleton got a paint job. At this time, an elevator was installed to take visitors up through the pedestal to the base of the spiral staircases. Starting in 1937, the

The Statue of Liberty has been maintained by the National Park Service since 1933.

THE SYMBOL OF LIBERTY

Although the American people were slow to come up with the money to build the pedestal for Liberty, they were quick to accept her into their hearts as an enduring symbol of what the United States stands for. The principle of liberty was one of the things that people fought for and achieved in the American Revolution, and it is one of the reasons that people from all over the world have immigrated to the United States. It is fitting that the statue itself is a kind of immigrant, born in the back streets and workshops of Paris. Since Liberty was erected in 1886, the statue has become one of our country's most enduring symbols, a reminder of the ideals that we hold dear.

Copies of the statue appear around the country and around the world. The largest replica of Liberty stands on top of a warehouse in New York City. This 55-foot-tall Liberty was built for a Russian immigrant who had prospered in the United States and wanted to show his appreciation of freedom and liberty. Other copies of Liberty stand in Hiroshima and Nagasaki, Japan, where the United States dropped atomic bombs at the end of World War II. In these bomb-scarred cities, Liberty stands for peace and understanding between countries.

Other replica statues have been erected in Paris, France; Hanoi, Vietnam; as well

World War I *Liberty bond poster*

statue had to be closed for almost two years, while the supports for the rays of Liberty's crown were replaced.

For many years, visitors covered the inside of the statue with graffiti. The worst of it was done with lipstick because lipstick penetrated the metal framework. In 1946, the interior of the statue was painted once again, this time with paint that was resistant to lipstick. Over the years, many little jobs were done to try and keep Liberty in shape.

as many other places around the United States. In 1989, a 27-foot-tall Liberty was erected by protesters in Tiananmen Square in Beijing, China. Their revolt against the government was brutally beaten down, but the ideals they were fighting for were made clear by their choice of Liberty as their symbol.

Liberty shows up in all sorts of places. One pair of collectors has more than 500 different Liberty post-cards, while another Liberty fan paid over $100,000 for one of the original replica statues made by Bartholdi to raise money for the construction. Liberty has appeared on numerous stamps in the United States and on 140 stamps in 35 countries around the world. In World Wars I and II, she was the symbol of what Americans were fighting for and was used to help sell war bonds. In fact, the war bonds were called Liberty bonds to remind those at home what their friends and relatives were fighting for overseas.

There have even been some who have suggested that the official symbol of the United States should be

Liberty made by Chinese demonstrators in May 1989

changed from the bald eagle to the Statue of Liberty. They argue that the eagle stands for power and force, while Liberty stands for peace and freedom. With her first hundred years behind her, there is one thing that is certain: the Statue of Liberty will continue to be one of the most recognized symbols of America throughout the world.

In addition to trying to maintain Liberty, other changes took place over the years. Various attempts were made to illuminate the torch and both the inside and outside of the statue. In 1956, the name of the statue's home base—Bedloe's Island—was officially changed to Liberty Island. In 1972, the American Museum of Immigration was opened there, but it was later closed when Ellis Island's Great Hall was restored and opened as a national museum in 1990.

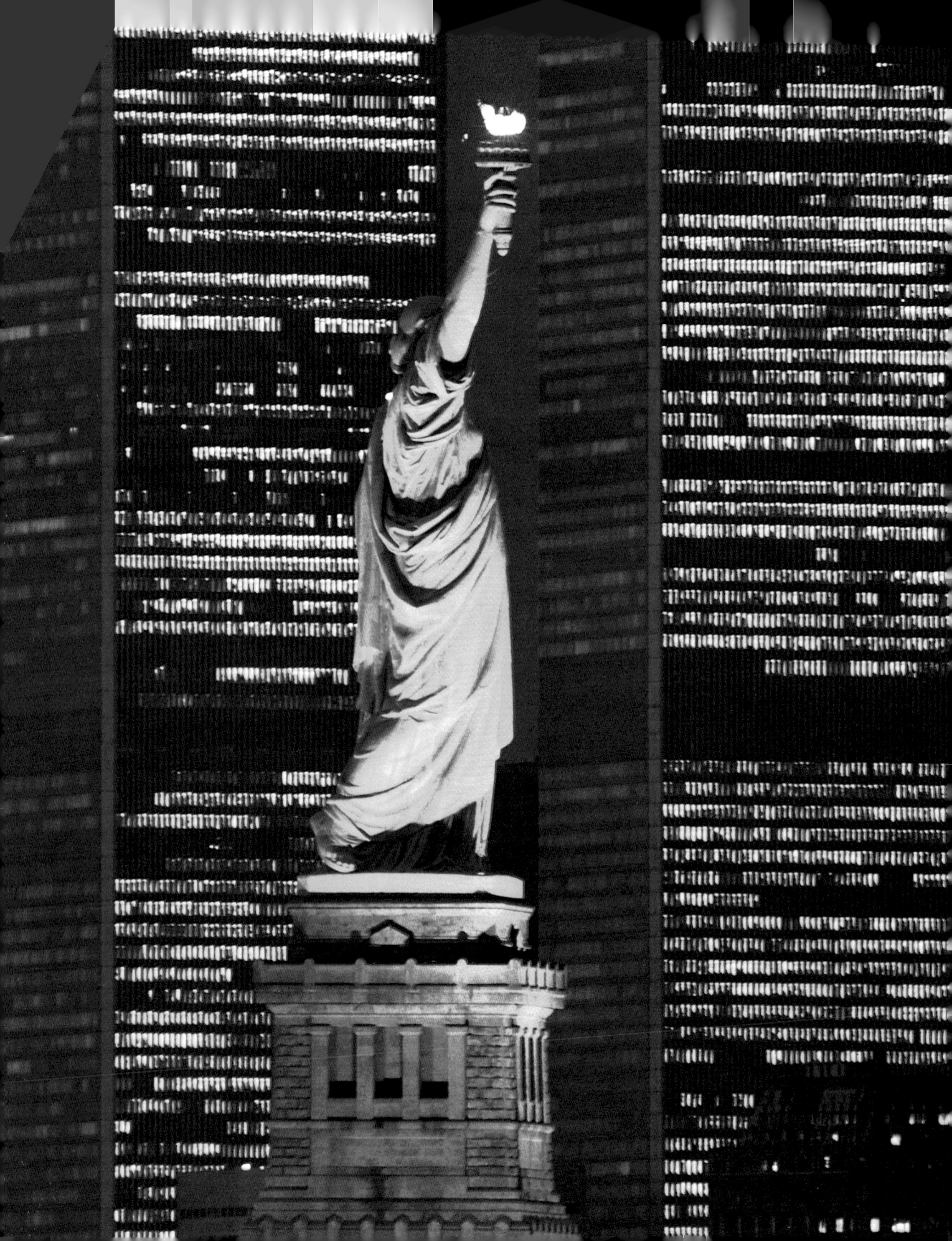

Liberty Gets a Face-Lift

By the 1980s, despite all the attention Liberty had received, the statue was in need of a major restoration. Much of the inspiration to restore Liberty came when people began to think about celebrating the statue's 100th birthday. A survey of the statue by a group of engineers revealed some alarming problems. Twenty-five-thousand rivets were either missing or loose, and many of the iron straps holding the copper sheets had corroded so badly that they were half their original thickness. The torch was so corroded that pieces were falling off.

Opposite:
Liberty creates
a dramatic
scene against
the nighttime
backdrop of the
World Trade
Center towers.

35

In addition to the problems caused by time, the survey discovered that the right arm and torch had been improperly installed when the statue was reassembled in 1886. The joints where the frame for the arm joined the main frame were weakened as a result and were in danger of failing. Liberty's head had also been put on incorrectly and was two feet off center. This caused one of the rays from the crown to rub against the right arm, and a hole had resulted in the copper skin in this area. The restoration of Liberty would have to be extensive if the statue was going to survive.

"If You Still Believe in Me, Save Me"

Ellis Island—the huge immigration center that had been the entry point into the United States for millions of people—was added to the Statue of Liberty National Monument in 1965, and it too was now in need of a massive restoration. President Ronald Reagan felt that both the Statue of Liberty and Ellis Island should be restored, however, he did not want to spend federal money on the projects. Reagan set up a commission to raise the $167 million that was first estimated to be needed for restorations.

The commission was made up of prominent Americans: Business leaders, politicians, entertainers, and labor union officials were all asked to serve. Lee Iacocca, the chairman of the board of the Chrysler Corporation was asked to lead the commission. Iaccoca had a special interest in the project, as his parents had both entered the United States through Ellis Island. When the final estimates were in, the commission was faced with the task of raising

ELLIS ISLAND

Unless you are part of the less-than-one percent of the U.S. population that is descended from Native Americans, you or your ancestors immigrated to the United States. During the last decades of the 19th century and the first half of the 20th century, there was a continuous flow of immigrants into America. During that

Immigrants looking at Liberty

time, almost half of all the immigrants entered the United States by ship, passing the Statue of Liberty on their way to Ellis Island, just a short way up the harbor from Liberty.

From its opening in 1892 until it was closed in 1954, Ellis Island was the busiest immigration center in the country, processing as many as 5,000 people a day. More than 16 million people from 120 different ethnic groups passed through the halls of Ellis Island over the years and many later became citizens of the United States.

After the Immigration and Naturalization Service abandoned Ellis Island in 1954, it fell into disrepair. When the government decided to turn the island into a museum, it realized that approximately $127 million would be needed to restore the buildings and create a museum of immigration. The foundation that raised the money to refurbish Liberty also raised the money for Ellis Island. In 1990, the island was rededicated as a museum that celebrates the ethnic diversity of the people who have come to the United States seeking the opportunities that Liberty symbolizes.

Then: Immigrants arrive at Ellis Island around the turn of the century.

Now: The renovated immigrant registry building houses the Ellis Island Immigration Museum.

$230 million to cover the costs of Liberty's make-over, future maintenance, and the 100th birthday celebration, as well as the restoration of Ellis Island.

Unlike the problems that the Franco-American Union had had raising the money for the pedestal in the 1880s, money flowed in to the Statue of Liberty–Ellis Island Centennial Foundation. The official slogan was "If You Still Believe in Me, Save Me!," and corporate America wanted to reap the benefits of being a part of such a patriotic undertaking. American Express, Coca-Cola, Westinghouse, Johnson and Johnson, and many other companies became official sponsors of the restoration and were licensed to use the Centennial Foundation's seal in their advertising. Many organizations, such as the Daughters of the American Revolution, the Freemasons, and the Knights of Columbus, also contributed to the statue's repair.

Three-quarters of the restoration money came from companies and organizations, the remainder came from private individuals and schoolchildren across the country. An elementary school in Florida built an eight-foot-tall papier-mâché replica of Liberty, held a walk-a-thon, and raised almost $12,000. An Arizona elementary school put on a three-mile "Liberty run" and sent in almost $2,500 for Liberty. During the 100 years that Liberty had stood on her island, the statue had become one of the most recognizable symbols of the United States, and many people wanted to see the statue endure.

This tall ship parade and the Statue of Liberty were both major parts of New York City's celebration of the bicentennial on July 4, 1976.

The actual restoration work was almost as complex as the original building of the statue. A specially designed, 300-ton scaffolding was erected to surround the entire statue and its pedestal. The scaffolding was made of aluminum and designed to withstand the forces of a 100-mile-per-hour wind. This was fortunate because on September 27, 1985, Hurricane Gloria buffeted the project with winds of 73 miles per hour.

As the restoration proceeded, Liberty was given a special bath—only her fourth one in 100 years. This bath consisted of chemicals that were formulated to clean and protect Liberty's copper skin. In addition to cleaning and repairing the outside of the statue, the entire strapping system that held the 300 copper sheets was replaced with new straps made of a corrosion-resistant stainless steel.

The biggest job of the restoration was repairing Liberty's right arm and the torch. The engineers on the project used sophisticated computer imaging to determine the stresses on the framework of the arm and torch, and then they designed a new support out of a lighter, yet stronger, metal. Not only did the interior frame of the arm and torch need to be replaced, the skin of the torch had to be replaced as well. To do this, metal workers from France who still worked in the traditional style of repoussé were brought to New York to fashion a new torch.

Scaffolding surrounds Liberty in this photo taken in February 1984.

After the restoration, Liberty's new gilded torch glimmered in the sunshine.

To make the new torch, a plaster cast was first made of the old torch, and then copper sheets were hammered into the resulting mold—just as the workers at Gaget, Gauthier had done 100 years earlier. Over the years, a number of revisions had been made to the torch—glass panes had been installed and lighting had been added. Bartholdi had originally suggested that the torch be gilded, or covered in gold, so that it would reflect the sunlight. The people in charge of the restoration decided to follow his suggestion. The torch was first coated with nickel and then gold leaf was applied as the final layer.

Many improvements were also made for the benefit of the millions of tourists who visit Liberty Island. The stairways were widened and the rest platforms were improved, the building and dock were modernized, and the park was made as handicap-accessible as possible.

The Biggest Birthday Party Ever

While no longer the tallest human-made structure in 1986, Liberty was still the tallest statue in the world, and the leaders of the Centennial Foundation wanted to give her the largest 100th birthday party ever seen. By most accounts, they succeeded. U.S. President Ronald Reagan and French President François Mitterand led the ceremonies.

More than 30 countries sent historical sailing ships to participate in the celebration, and over 30,000 boats lined the harbor as the six-hour-long parade of tall ships and naval vessels from around the world passed by Liberty. There were concerts and parties throughout the city for three days leading up to the unveiling of the restored Liberty.

On the evening of July 3, 1986, the new lights on Liberty Island were turned on, and Liberty glowed as a nationwide audience watched the party on television. Many communities around the country had built replicas of Liberty and held their own celebrations. Tulsa, Oklahoma, built a papier-mâché Liberty; Memphis, Tennessee, made theirs out of cake; and Seattle, Washington, used Lego blocks to re-create the great green lady.

Finally, on July 4, 1986, Liberty's second 100 years as the symbol of American freedom began. Among the many festivities was the largest fireworks display in U.S. history. For the millions of Americans who witnessed it, the spirit of Liberty was alive and well.

Top: *Boats in "Operation Sail" helped celebrate Liberty's 100th birthday.* **Bottom:** *Fireworks explode over Liberty, July 4, 1986.*

The Statue of Liberty is one of
the most recognizable symbols of
New York City—and of America.

GLOSSARY

asbestos A form of magnesium silicate, once used for fireproofing, electrical insulation, building materials, brake linings, and chemical filters.

beveling A process in which the edge of a material is thinned at an angle that matches the corresponding edge of a piece of material to which it is to be connected.

butt joint A way of joining two pieces of material in which the edges of the material are lined up and then both are attached to the same thin strip of the same or similar material.

centennial Occurring once every 100 years; a centennial commemoration.

concrete A hard, strong construction material, consisting of sand and gravel mixed with mortar or cement.

constitution Fundamental principles of a government or a nation, either implied in its laws, institutions, and customs or embodied in one or more documents.

copper A soft, reddish brown metal that is an excellent conductor of heat and electricity and is widely used for electrical wiring and water piping.

coppersmith One who works or manufactures objects in copper.

derrick A machine for hoisting and moving heavy objects, consisting of a movable boom equipped with cables and pulleys and connected to the base of an upright stationary beam.

dovetail joint A way of connecting two pieces of material in which opposing patterns are cut in the edges of the material and then fitted together.

immigrant A person who leaves one country to settle permanently in another.

immigrate To enter and settle in a country or region where one was not born.

insulator A material that insulates or protects from sound, heat, or electricity.

lap joint A joining of two materials in which one piece overlaps the other.

lighthouse A tall structure topped by a powerful light used as a beacon or signal to help ships navigate.

monarchy Form of government in which one person (usually related to a previous monarch) rules, often for life.

monumental Impressively large, sturdy, and enduring.

pedestal An architectural support or base, as for a column or statue.

repoussé Shaped or decorated with patterns in relief formed by hammering and pressing on the reverse side; used especially with metal.

restoration An act of restoring or renovating.

rivet A metal bolt or pin having a head on one end that is inserted through aligned holes in pieces to be joined and then hammered on the plain end so as to form a second head.

sculptor One who shapes, molds, or fashions especially with artistry or precision.

shellac A liquid made from lac (the excretion of certain insects that is collected from the bark of trees) and widely used in varnishes and paints.

CHRONOLOGY

1865 Gift from the French people to the people of the United States first discussed at a dinner party hosted by Laboulaye with Bartholdi present.

1870 First model of the Statue of Liberty completed by Bartholdi.

1871 Bartholdi travels to the United States to explore the possible sites for the statue.

1875 Franco-American Union formed at a banquet held for the purpose and the first public announcement of the statue made.
Final model for the statue is presented.
Construction begins in Paris.
Bedloe's Island in New York Harbor is chosen as the site for the Statue of Liberty.

1876 Right arm and torch completed and sent to Philadelphia for display at the Philadelphia Centennial Exposition. Arm and torch are then sent to New York City for display.

1877 Eiffel becomes the engineer for the project.

1881 Skeleton of the statue is begun, and Liberty's big toe is the first part to be attached to the framework.

1882 Liberty completed to the waist.
Framework for the arm and torch is completed.
Arm and torch brought back to Paris for installation on the statue.
Richard Morris Hunt submits his design for the pedestal.

1883 **April**—The ground-breaking for the pedestal is held on Bedloe's Island.
August—Liberty's head installed.

October—Construction of the concrete foundation is begun.
Emma Lazarus's poem "The New Colossus" is published.

1884 August—The statue is completed at the workshop of Gaget, Gauthier, and Company in Paris.
Cornerstone for pedestal is laid.

1885 January 1—Bartholdi begins the process of taking the statue apart and preparing it for shipment.
One-quarter scale model of Liberty, cast in bronze, given to the people of Paris by a group of Americans living in the city.
May 21—Liberty leaves France from the port of Rouen aboard the Isère and arrives in New York on June 17.
Through the efforts of the New York World and its publisher Joseph Pulitzer, $100,000 is raised to help build the pedestal for Liberty.

1886 Pedestal completed and the statue reassembled.
October 28—The dedication ceremony is held.

1956 Name of Bedloe's Island changed to Liberty Island.

1981 Committee formed and publishes a report on the condition of the statue.

1983 Fund-raising for the Statue of Liberty and Ellis Island restorations begins.

1984 July 4—as part of the restoration, the top half of the torch is removed to be rebuilt.

1986 Restoration completed.
July 3 and 4—rededication ceremonies are held.

FURTHER READING

Coerr, Eleanor. *Lady with a Torch: How the Statue of Liberty Was Born*. New York: Harper and Row, 1986.

Glassman, Bruce. *New York*. Woodbridge, CT: Blackbirch Press, 1991.

Kallen, Stuart A. *Statue of Liberty: The New Colossus*. Minneapolis, MN: Abdo and Daughters, 1994.

Miller, Natalie. *The Statue of Liberty*. Chicago: Childrens Press, 1993.

Penner, Lucille R. *Statue of Liberty*. New York: Random House, 1994.

Shapiro, Mary J. *How They Built the Statue of Liberty*. New York: Random House, 1985.

Sorensen, Lynda. *Statue of Liberty*. Vero Beach, FL: Rourke, 1994.

SOURCE NOTES

Allen, Frederic. "Saving the Statue." *American Heritage*. June–July 84, 97–109.

Bell, James B. and Richard I. Abrams. *In Search of Liberty: The Story of the Statue of Liberty and Ellis Island*. Garden City, N.Y.: Doubleday & Co., 1984.

Davidson, Spencer. "Liberty Primps for That Great Big Birthday Party." *Smithsonian*, June 1986, 68–75.

Hall, Alice J. "Liberty Lights Her Lamp Once More," *National Geographic*, July 1986, 2–19.

Harris, Jonathan. *A Statue for America: The First 100 Years of the Statue of Liberty*. New York: Four Winds Press, 1985.

Hayden, Richard Seth. *Restoring the Statue of Liberty: Sculpture, Structure, Symbol*. New York: McGraw-Hill Book Co., 1986.

Holzer, Harold. "A Hundred Fourths of July Rolled into One," *America History Illustrated*, June 1986, 38–46.

Kleiger, Estelle F. "Emma Lazarus: 'I Lift my Lamp Beside the Golden Door!'," *American History Illustrated*, June 1986, 30–33.

"Liberty at 100," *Life*, July 1986, 47–68.

Martz, Larry and Martin Kasindorf and Peter McKillop. "A Party for the Lady," *Newsweek*, July 7, 1986, 14–17.

Mercer, Charles. *Statue of Liberty*. New York: G.P. Putnam's Sons, 1979.

O'Connor, Colleen and Andrew Murr. "Securing Liberty Weekend," *Newsweek*, June 23, 1986, 32.

Peterson, Ivars. "Lessons Learned from a Lady," *Science News*, December 20 & 27, 1986, 392–395.

Przygoda, Nancy. "Security Fit for a Lady," *Security Management*, April 1994, 32.

Schamel, W. B. "Teaching with Documents," *Social Education*, September 1992, 299.

"The Spirit of '86," *Newsweek*, July 14, 1986, 21–27.

Stengel, Richard. "The Lady's Party," *Time*, July 14, 1986, 10–20.

Trachtenberg, Marvin. *The Statue of Liberty*. New York: Viking Press, 1976.

INDEX

American Museum of Immigration, 33, 37

American Revolution, 5–6, 32

Asbestos, 16

Bartholdi, Frédéric-Auguste, 23, 24, 40
  biographical sketch of, 10
  and construction phase, 7, 9, 12, 13, 14
  at dedication, 29, 30
  and idea for Statue of Liberty, 6–7
  replica statues by, 33
  selection of site by, 19–20
  and Statue of Liberty as a symbol, 11

Bartholdi (steamboat), 25

Bedloe's Island, 7, 19–20, 33.
  See also Liberty Island

Beveling, 15–16

Centennial Celebration
  (Philadelphia, 1876), 6, 9–10

China, 33

Cleveland, Grover, 22, 25, 30

Concrete, 23–24

Congress, appropriation by, 25

Copper
  and construction phase, 11, 13, 14, 15, 16
  donation of, 7
  and reassembling phase, 28
  and restoration, 35, 36, 39, 40

Coppersmiths, 14, 15

Crown, 33, 36

Declaration of Independence, 6, 9, 10

Dedication ceremony, 25, 29–31

Derricks, 25, 27–28

Dispatch (U.S. ship), 30

Eiffel, Alexandre-Gustave, 10, 11–12, 14

Elevators, 31

Ellis Island, 33, 36, 37

Evarts, William M., 20, 30

Financing. *See* Congress; fund-raising

Fingers, 14

Fort Wood, 20, 24–25

Frame
  iron, 11, 12, 14, 16, 27, 28
  wooden, 13

France
  construction phase in, 9–17
  fund-raising in, 7, 10, 11, 13
  replicas of Statue of Liberty in, 32
  Statue of Liberty as gift from, 5–7

Franco-American Union, 7, 30

Fund-raising
  for Ellis Island, 36, 37
  in France, 7, 10, 11, 13
  for maintenance, 38
  for 100th birthday celebration, 38
  for pedestal, 20, 21–23, 25
  and replica statues, 33
  for restoration purposes, 36, 37, 38
  in United States, 20, 21–23, 25, 33, 36, 37, 38

Gaget, Gauthier, and Company, 9, 13, 14, 16, 29

Governor's Island, 19

Graffiti, 33

Granite, 25, 31

Head, 13, 16, 36

Hunt, Richard Morris, 23, 25

Iacocca, Lee, 36

Île des Cygnes, France, 25

Immigration, 20–21, 32, 37

Insulation, 16

Iron frame, 11, 12, 14, 16, 27, 28

Isère (French ship), 27

Japan, 32
Japy Fréres, 7
Joints, 15, 16, 36

Laboulaye, Edouard-René
     Lefebvre de, 6–7, 10–11, 30
Lazarus, Emma, 20–21
Lesseps, Ferdinand-Marie de, 30
Liberty Island, 33, 40, 41
Lighthouse Board, 31
Lightning, 28
Lipstick, 33

Maintenance, of Statue of Liberty,
     31–33
Memphis, Tennessee, 41
Mitterand, François, 41

National Park Service, 31
"The New Colossus" (Lazarus), 20–21

Painting, of Statue of Liberty, 31, 33
Paris Universal Exposition (1878), 13
Pedestal, construction of, 19–25
Pulitzer, Joseph, 22–23

Reagan, Ronald, 36, 41
Reassembling, of Statue of Liberty,
     25, 27–28
Repoussé, 13, 39
Rivets, 15–16, 28, 35
Robe, 17

Scaffolding, 39
Seattle, Washington, 41

Shellac, 16
Site selection, 7, 19–21
Staircase, 30–31, 40
Stamps, Statue of Liberty on, 33
Statue of Liberty
     construction of, 7, 9–17
     dedication of, 25, 29–31
     disassembling the, 25
     maintaining the, 31–33
     100th birthday of, 35, 38, 40–41
     reassembling of, 25, 27–28
     replicas/miniatures of, 22, 25,
        29–30, 32, 41
     restoration of, 35–41
     site of, 7, 19–21
     size of, 11
     as a symbol, 5, 7, 11, 21, 22,
        32–33, 38
Statue of Liberty (France), 25
Statue of Liberty-Ellis Island
     Centennial Foundation, 36, 37,
     38, 40–41
Stone, Charles P., 24
Strapping system, 39

Tall ships, 41
Tiananmen Square (Beijing, China), 33
Toe, 17
Torch and right arm, 9–10, 13, 14,
     16–17, 33, 35, 36, 39–40
Tulsa, Oklahoma, 41

Vietnam, 32

War bonds, 33
War Department, U.S., 31
Wooden frames, 13